Black's Sketchbooks

London Adam & Charles Black

PUBLISHED BY
A. & C. BLACK · SOHO SQUARE · LONDON W.

THE THAMES

A SKETCH-BOOK BY
R. SHARPLEY.

A & C BLACK L^{TD} LONDON W

LIST OF SKETCHES
BY
R. SHARPLEY.

STRAND·ON·THE·GREEN _   R.SHARPLEY.

KEW BRIDGE —   R. SHARPLEY.

FERRY ROAD . TWICKENHAM   R.SHARPLEY -

KINGSTON . YE OLDE CURIOSITY SHOPPE .   R SHARPLEY .

HAMPTON COURT —   R. SHARPLEY.

SUNBURY .   R. SHARPLEY -

WALTON BRIDGE —   R·SHARPLEY·

BELOW STAINES BRIDGE —   R. SHARPLEY.

WINDSOR CASTLE AND BRIDGE —   R·S·

IN BRAY VILLAGE _   R.S.

IN WEST STREET . MARLOW .   R. SHARPLEY .

" YE OLDE BELL INN . HURLEY .   R.S .

HURLEY _ THE OLD BARN and DOVECOT _ R·SHARPLEY _

HOUSE BOATS AT HENLEY —   R. SHARPLEY —

SONNING FROM THE BRIDGE —   R. CHAPPLEY —

MAPLEDURHAM MILL —

R.S —

GORING . THE BRIDGE .   R. SHARPLEY .

STREATLEY MILL.   R. SHARPLEY.

WALLINGFORD –   R.SHARPLEY –

SHILLINGFORD BRIDGE.   R. SHARPLEY.

DORCHESTER ABBEY - SOUTH DOOR -   R.S.

ABINGDON BRIDGE —   R SHARPLEY —

AT IFFLEY —

R.S.

First published in Great Britain in 1921
by A&C Black Publishers
36 Soho Square
London W1D 3QY
www.acblack.com

This edition published 2009

© 1921, 2009 A&C Black

ISBN 978-1-408-11556-5

A CIP record of this book is available from the British Library

Printed and bound in China